Hassan Abdulrazzak

LOVE, BOMBS AND APPLES

includes
The Several Beheadings of Ashraf Fayadh

D1306329

OBERON BOOKS
LONDON

WWW.OBERONBOOKS.COM

First published in 2016 by Oberon Books Ltd

521 Caledonian Road, London N7 9RH

Tel: +44 (0) 20 7607 3637 / Fax: +44 (0) 20 7607 3629

e-mail: info@oberonbooks.com

www.oberonbooks.com

Copyright © Hassan Abdulrazzak, 2016

Hassan Abdulrazzak is hereby identified as author of these plays in accordance with section 77 of the Copyright, Designs and Patents Act 1988. The author has asserted his moral rights.

All rights whatsoever in this play are strictly reserved and application for performance etc. should be made before commencement of rehearsal to The Artists Partnership, 101 Finsbury Pavement, London, EC2A 1RS, UK. No performance may be given unless a licence has been obtained, and no alterations may be made in the title or the text of the play without the author's prior written consent.

You may not copy, store, distribute, transmit, reproduce or otherwise make available this publication (or any part of it) in any form, or binding or by any means (print, electronic, digital, optical, mechanical, photocopying, recording or otherwise), without the prior written permission of the publisher. Any person who does any unauthorized act in relation to this publication may be liable to criminal prosecution and civil claims for damages.

A catalogue record for this book is available from the British Library.

PB ISBN: 9781783198245

E ISBN: 9781783198252

Cover design by topright design limited (www.topright.co.uk)

Printed and bound by 4EDGE Ltd., Essex, United Kingdom.

Visit www.oberonbooks.com to read more about all our books and to buy them. You will also find features, author interviews and news of any author events, and you can sign up for e-newsletters so that you're always first to hear about our new releases.

Contents

LOVE, BOMBS AND APPLES

To Ceci

PREFACE

I had the pleasure of meeting Hassan Abdulrazzak during my third year at RADA in 2009. My teacher, Lloyd Trott, kindly asked him to write a monologue for me to perform for my showcase called *The Tree*. Within a few days, Hassan sent me a five-page monologue titled *Love in the time of barriers*. This became the first of the characters in *Love, Bombs & Apples*. The writing was brilliantly relevant, funny and political. Unfortunately I could only perform two minutes of it for my showcase, but I loved Hassan's writing and at some point in the future wanted to perform the whole piece.

Cut to 2014. I got in touch with Hassan asking if he'd like to meet for a coffee and discuss the possibility of doing a full-length version of *Love in the Time of Barriers*. During our coffee and chat in the sun at Covent Garden, Hassan showed me two other pieces titled *Level 42* and *The Apple* and we discussed the possibility of doing a show using all three pieces. We also brainstormed possible directors we'd like to work with. Enter Rosamunde Hutt, a wonderful director I had worked with previously on an adaptation of *The Snow Queen*. The team grew further with the addition of James Hesford (Sound Designer), Mila Sanders (Designer) and Charlotte Cunningham (Turtle Key Arts) and so did the script when Hassan said 'I've thought of an idea for a fourth piece!' (*Landing Strip*).

Having sent the whole play to the Arcola's PlayWROUGHT Festival, it was selected as one of twelve new plays, which would be performed as a reading in January 2015. This was a great opportunity to test the format in front of a live audience and led to a week run at the Arcola as part of the Shubbak Festival.

Now in 2016, we have an exciting few months ahead taking the show around the country and returning for a full four weeks at the Arcola Theatre. It's been an absolute pleasure working on *Love, Bombs & Apples*. As an actor it's a dream to work on such fabulous writing with a talented and generous team of people.

Asif Khan, May 2016.

ACKNOWLEDGMENTS

So many people helped us along the way.
Thank you to all the following:

Munira Albayaty, Jenny Bakst, Iain Bloomfield,
Shenagh Cameron, Andrew Charity, Nick
Connaughton, Elyse Dodgson, Mehmet Ergen, Amy
Evans, Imad Farajin, Norman Finkelstein, Daniel
Gorman, Stacey Gregg, Shiv Grewal, Cecilia Guevara,
Sally Hague, Saad Hussain, Fin Kennedy, Nicolas
Kent, Asra Khan, Cristina Malcolmson, Tim Marriot,
Leyla Nazli, Jake Pike, Sophie Postlethwaite, Clemmie
Reynolds, Asil Robertson, James Robertson, Richard
Ryder, Aser el Saqqa, Eckhard Thiemann, Lloyd Trott.

All the staff at Arcola theatre, Banipal Magazine,
The Iraqi Cultural Centre, Graeae, Kali Theatre, The
Richard Carne Trust, RADA, Royal Court Theatre,
Roxane Vacca Management, Shubbak festival, Tamasha
Theatre Co and Tara Arts

And our families.

Love, Bombs & Apples was first commissioned and produced by AIK Productions. World premiere was at the Arcola Theatre, London, as part of the Shubbak Festival, July 2015. AIK Productions & Turtle Key Arts co-produced the UK national tour in 2016.

Producers	AIK Productions and Turtle Key Arts
Writer	Hassan Abdulrazzak
Director	Rosamunde Hutt
Performer	Asif Khan
Set & Costume Designer	Mila Sanders
Sound Design	James Hesford
Lighting Design	Charlie Lucas
Voice Coach	Richard Ryder
Technical Stage Manager	Joe Myles
Covering Technical Stage Manager	Stacey Choudhury-Potter
Company Stage Manager	Ella Dixon
Marketing	Turtle Key Arts
Press	Media Moguls
Filming & Editing	Primo Digital Video Productions
Graphic Design	topright.co.uk
Photography	Mila Sanders

Tues 10 & Weds 11 May 7.45pm
Northern Stage, Newcastle
0191 230 5151

Fri 13 & Sat 14 May 8pm
Mercury Theatre, Colchester
01206 573 948

Tues 17 & Weds 18 May 7.45pm
Printers Playhouse, Eastbourne
01323 301 250

Thurs 19 & Fri 20 May 8pm
Attenborough Arts Centre, Leicester
0116 252 2455

Weds 25 & Thurs 26 May 7.45pm
Cast, Doncaster
01302 303 959

Tues 31 May – Sat 25 June (Excl Suns) 8pm
Sat Matinees 3.30pm
Arcola, London
020 7503 1646

Weds 29 & Thurs 30 June 7.45pm
York Theatre Royal
01904 623 568

Fri 1 & Sat 2 July 7.30pm
Theatre in the Mill, Bradford
01274 233 200

Mon 11, Tues 12 & Weds 13 July 7.30pm
Oldham Coliseum Theatre Studio
0161 624 2829

Thurs 21 & Fri 22 July 7.30pm
Bluecoat, Arabica Festival Liverpool
0151 702 5324

BIOGRAPHIES

ASIF KHAN Performer and Co Producer

Asif trained at The Royal Academy Of Dramatic Art (RADA), where he won a Laurence Olivier Bursary Award.

Theatre includes: Handbagged (UK Tour 2015, Tricycle Theatre/Eleanor Lloyd Productions), Love, Bombs & Apples (Arcola Theatre 2015), Punjabi Boy (RichMix), Multitudes (Tricycle Theatre), The Nutcracker & The Mouse King (Unicorn Theatre), The Book (Flying Cloud), Queen of the Nile (HullTruck), Kabaddi Kabaddi Kabaddi (Arcola Theatre), The Snow Queen (Unicorn Theatre/ Trestle) and in Snookered (Tamasha/ Bush Theatre), which was nominated for 'Best New Play' & 'Best Ensemble Cast' by Off West End Theatre Awards 2012, and Won 'Best New Play' at the Manchester Theatre Awards.

Also: Mixed Up North (Out of Joint), Malvolio in Twelfth Night (National Theatre), Playback (Ankur Productions); and Three Sisters, Rookery Nook, The Last Days of Judas Iscariot, Julius Caesar, Antigone, The Glass Menagerie at RADA.

Recent screen work includes: Love Type D (Feature film to be released in 2016), Spooks (Series 10), The Dumping Ground, Doctors, Casualty (BBC). Dark Matters, Terry Pratchett's Going Postal for Sky1, Man Down & Bradford Riots (Channel 4) and 'Plot to Bring Down Britain's Planes' (BAFTA Winner).

As a writer Asif's first full-length play COMBUSTION, was selected as one of 6 new plays for the Arcola Theatre's playWROUGHT#2 Festival, 2014. It also progressed through to the final stage of the BBC Writers Room Script Room 8 Scheme. His piece TIGHT BASTARDS was performed as a reading at the Soho Theatre for Tamasha Theatre (2015) and at Theatre503 (2016). Asif was recently commissioned to write a play on the theme of Migration by Tamasha & The Migration Museum for Landau Forte College, Derby.

He was nominated for the ADOPT A PLAYWRIGHT AWARD (OffWestEnd.Com) and made it through to the final shortlist.

ROSAMUNDE HUTT Director

Rosamunde has led or co-led three major companies (Hijinx Theatre 1990-1993; Theatre Centre, Director, 1993-2007 and Unicorn, Associate Artistic Director, 2007-2011). Since 2011 her international work includes touring Anupama Chandrasekhar's The Snow Queen to India (Trestle Theatre/British Council), co-leading workshops on young people's theatre in Japan and directing Charles Way's The Snow Queen in Romania, now in repertoire and shown on Romanian National Television on Christmas Day 2015 (Theatre Ion Creanga).

Her 2013/15 credits include productions of classics and new plays at RADA, ALRA, East 15 (including The Workroom by Jean-Claude Grumberg, in an English translation by Amy Rosenthal, Arcola 2016), Nottingham Playhouse (Grandpa in my Pocket-Teamwork by Mellie Buse and Jan Page), AJTC/ York Theatre Royal (Bin Men by Mike Kenny), Polka Theatre (Alice's Adventures in Wonderland by Simon Reade and Operation Magic Carpet by Samantha Ellis), and a site specific new play for Dragon Breath Theatre (A Crack in Time by Peter Rumney).

She directed the showcase for Goldsmiths MA Writers in 2015 at Soho Theatre and regularly helps develop new plays for Kali Theatre. In April 2016 she was invited to speak about her work commissioning new writing for young audiences at the Youth Theatre Festival 2016 in Athens (Onassis Cultural Centre) and she will be directing actor/writer Michael Mears in his new play This Evil Thing at the Edinburgh Festival this year.

HASSAN ABDULRAZZAK Writer

Hassan is of Iraqi origin, born in Prague and living in London. He holds a PhD in molecular biology and has worked at Harvard and Imperial College.

Hassan's first play Baghdad Wedding, was staged at Soho Theatre in 2007 to great acclaim. It went on to have productions in Australia and India and was also broadcast on BBC radio 3. Hassan's play The Prophet was performed at The Gate Theatre in 2012 and was based on extensive interviews in Cairo with revolutionaries and soldiers, journalists and cab drivers. More recently he was commissioned by the Kevin Spacey Foundation to write Dhow Under The Sun, a play for 35 young actors, which was staged in Sharjah, UAE (Jan 2015). He was also commissioned by Untold Theatre to write Catalina, the story of the Moorish slave of Catherine of Aragon (Ovalhouse Theatre 1-4 April 2015).

His short plays include The Tale Of Sindbad And The Old Goat which was part of a multi-author-show called Arab Nights that was performed at Soho Theatre in 2012 and later toured the UK and Lost Kingdom which was selected out of 75 scripts to be part of San Francisco's Golden Thread ReOrient 2015 festival.

Hassan has received the George Devine, Meyer-Whitworth and Pearson theatre awards as well as the Arab British Centre Award for Culture.

MILA SANDERS Costume and Set Design

Mila trained at the University of Wales, Aberystwyth and Wimbledon School of Art.

Her designs include: Darknet (Southwark Playhouse), Soapbox (Talawa), The Flannelettes (Kings Head), Game of Life (The Yard), Queen of the Nile (Hull Truck), Dogs Barking (RADA), Parallax, The Door Never Closes, All the Little Things We Crushed (Almeida), The Only Way is Chelsea's (Root Theatre/ York Theatre Royal), The Rite of Spring / Romeo and Juliet (Concert Theatre), Snakes and Ladders (Rolemop), Jelly Bean Jack (Little Angel), Pub Quiz (New Writing North), A Midsummer Night's Dream (NT Education).

As Costume Designer: Macbeth, Twelfth Night (NT Discover), Tombstone Tales and Boothill Ballads (Arcola), Jason and the Argonauts (BAC and tour), Unfolding Andersen (Theatre-rites).

CHARLIE LUCAS Lighting Designer

Charlie's lighting designs include Bully Boy (Colchester Mercury), As You Like It (Southwark Playhouse), I Loved Lucy, The First Man, Flowers of the Forest, Fever, Ivy and Joan (Jermyn Street), The Match Box (Liverpool Playhouse & Tricycle), Rise Up, The Muddy Choir, Advice for the Young at Heart (Theatre Centre, touring), Equally Divided, Mother Goose (Watford Palace), Von Ribbentrop's Watch (Oxford Playhouse), Frozen, Archimedes Principle (Park Theatre), Jealousy (The Print Room), Dirty Great Love Story (Soho & off-Broadway), Red Riding Hood (Theatre Royal Stratford East), Walking the Tightrope, In Blood: The Bacchae (Arcola), Blue Remembered Hills (New Diorama Theatre), Cautionary Tales (Opera North), The Magic Flute (Garsington Opera at West Green House), Werther (Opera Les Azuriales, Nice), Oberon (New Sussex Opera), Un Ballo in Maschera, The Return of Ulysses, La Rondine, La Traviata, Acis and Galatea (Iford Arts). Charlie trained at RADA.

JAMES HESFORD Sound Designer & Composer

James originally comes from Yorkshire and established himself as a leading jazz musician in London in the 1970s. In 1980 he won the Arts Council GLAA Young Jazz Musician of the Year.

He recorded his first Album for EMI Records at Abbey Road Studios. James is founder and leader of the WCMO (Working Classical Music Orchestra) the PGO (Pocket Guerrilla Orchestra) and Cellorhythmics. James has composed for contemporary classical music ensembles, Theatre, Film and TV. Recent work includes: World premiere Citerna & Sham Shui Po Circles for 12 pianos at the Royal Festival Hall, Channel 4, pick of the week documentary Sex, Lies and Parkinson's, National Lottery Theme BBC, Michael Parkinson – Talkshow Story, David Almond's Heaven Eyes, Kali's (Asian Women's Theatre) Gandhi and Coconuts, Kensington Palace documentary commission Victoria and Albert.

TURTLE KEY ARTS Co-Producers

Turtle Key Arts unlocks creative potential in individuals, companies and communities, producing and devising original, ground-breaking, inclusive art to entertain and inspire.

As creative producers they enable each project to reach its full artistic potential and ensure that participation and education is embedded at the heart of everything they do.

Their work has a UK and international reach through a wide variety of innovative projects with many different collaborators and partners, currently including the companies: Ockham's Razor, RedCape Theatre, Amici Dance Theatre Company, Joli Vyann, Slot Machine and SMITH dancetheatre; and recent collaborations with: English Touring Opera, Royal College of Music, The Wigmore Hall, National Portrait Gallery, Opera North, The Royal Court Theatre, Lyric Hammersmith and Oxford University.

They have played a committed role in advancing participation in the arts by disabled, disadvantaged and socially excluded people, and are widely recognised as a leader in this eld, often charting new territories, such as Turtle Song for people with Dementia and The Key Club for young people with Autism.

Turtle Key Arts was formed in 1989 as a unique and ground-breaking accessible space; and accessibility for all continues to be a key philosophy of the company. www.turtlekeyarts.org.uk

TURTLE KEY ARTS STAFF:

Artistic Director: Charlotte Cunningham
Chief Executive: Alison King
Marketing & Development Director: Shaun Dawson

Producer: Holly Cameron-Jennings
Finance Manager: Alan Bowyer
Education Manager: Ruth Naylor-Smith

Production Assistant: Imogen Collacott

Supported by Arts Council England, The Iraqi Cultural Centre, The Richard Carne Trust, Shubbak Festival and Arcola Theatre.

1. LOVE IN THE TIME OF BARRIERS

[Inspired by a true story told to the author by Palestinian actor / playwright Imad Farajin]

Sex. It's such a problem, isn't it? Don't you find? Even when you're famous, as I nearly am, it still is.

> *Beat.*

Not that long ago, I was playing Hamlet at Al-Kasaba Theatre in Ramallah. The actor playing Claudius was chosen because he looked like the spitting image of president Mahmoud Abbas.

You might remember Mahmoud Abbas from such capitulations as his condemnation of Hamas while the citizens of Gaza were busy dodging white phosphorous.

> *Makes explosion sound.*

My favourite scene is when I am in my mother's bedroom and letting her have it: 'Look here, upon this picture, and on this'…well I'm sure you know it.

I hold up a picture of Yasser Arafat– our great resistance leader who everybody here believes died because the Israelis poisoned him – and I say things like 'what a grace was seated on this brow'…and the audience is just lost in false memory.

I mean some of the intellectuals there would spit and curse if you so much as mentioned Arafat – on account of the small matter of him keeping a few million dollars of our money for himself and his cronies – but at that moment, when Gaza was being pulverised, they too lost themselves in the mythical past his photo represented.

Then I'd say to my mother: 'This was your husband. Look you now, what follows' and I hold up a picture of Mahmoud Abbas and I swear, every night, the hisses would come from the audience as if on cue.

The long and short of it is that I was electric, just bloody electric.

So after the last performance, we have the mother of all parties in the basement of the theatre. And I'm shaking hands left, right and centre. Cultural attaché of this, arts director of that. Just a sea of handshakes and cards thrust my way and pats on the back and bottles of Taybeh beer flying towards me. I begin to feel the muscles of my face straining from all the fake smiling and I'm dying for a cigarette so at the first lull, I make for the stairs then out the door.

Lights up a cigarette, takes a puff.

Heaven.

Beat.

Then I hear this woman's voice. 'Can you light mine?' I turn around to see this gorgeous, gorgeous girl, cropped hair, green, almost phosphorous eyes, like those of a cat's, dressed in some sexy, I don't know what it was: Chanel, maybe Versace dress. The kind of dress that says if you don't have a Platinum card in your wallet, don't bother saying hello.

Beat.

Except it was her saying hello to me. When she put the cigarette between her lips and tilted her head towards me, I swear it took every effort not to look down..

Looks down at his crotch.

…you know, just to make sure Big Brother wasn't ripping a hole through my jeans.

Turns out she's English. Studies political something or other at a place called: SO-ASS? And was here to research her MA. She'd had a little bit too much to drink and kept spilling her vodka and apologising and spilling and apologising which made me realize the odds on us having sex were pretty good.

See, sex is very difficult here, it really is. You have three basic options: go to a prostitute, not my style. Get married young, which is the path most guys take but no way am I getting married now. Are you crazy? I'll get married when I have Robert De Niro's number on speed dial. Oh yes, you better fucking believe it. I'm going all the way from Ramallah to LA.

Anything less is simply unacceptable, darling.

Beat.

The third option – we're back on sex in case you're getting lost – the third option is to find a foreign girl. Perhaps someone working for the thousand and one NGOs we have here. But most of them stick to their own. The adventurous ones, who like to dip their fingers in our local dishes so to speak, are harder to find. This one is clearly up for it.

She tells me her name but because of the background noise, I don't catch it. In my mind I begin to call her: Chanel girl.

Beat.

As she starts to tell me all about herself, my brain turns into a split screen. One side is nodding and laughing where appropriate and doing all that 'I'm taking interest in everything you're saying' bit, and I was, truly, well kind of, but the other side is thinking where the fuck can I take her to get laid?

This is not an easy problem to solve. I live with my mother, three sisters, two brothers and their respective wives and children. I can't give you an exact estimate of our household because I don't know who I'll find there every night when I get back. It's an animal thing, I guess. When your very existence is threatened, you have two options: extinction or breeding. So taking Chanel girl home is a definite no no.

After the party is over, we get in my car and I drive us around. She is staying in lodgings run by Franciscan nuns so sex there was going to be out of the question also. She tells me more about her life: private school in a place called Sorry? Her dissatisfaction with her privileged friends, her guilt about being privileged herself. I nod, make sounds of sympathy but all the time, one side of the split screen is busy computing all the possible places to get laid in Ramallah at this time of night.

Beat.

I secretly text few mates whilst she's talking but the replies are all the same: 'forget it', 'no chance' or my personal favourite: 'cut your losses and settle for a hand job.'

Beat.

Then I worry she's getting bored because I've been silent. So I try to make conversation. I tell her I like her dress. She says 'thank you'.

Is it Chanel, I ask? She laughs.

Versace? She laughs some more. What's so funny?

Then she tells me she got it in the sales from a place called Debbie-Hams? Which sounds like a food shop to me so I'm super confused but I laugh with her anyway, pretending I get the joke.

In my mind, I still call her Chanel girl.

She puts her bare feet on the dashboard. Man, she had this green toenail polish on which just drove me crazy – I'd like to give you some intellectual reason for my lust, like perhaps the green reminded me of the elusive peace we've been chasing but that would be a barefaced lie. It's at that point – while I'm thinking how callus-free and soft to the touch her feet must be that she starts to talk about the occupation, about the tears she has shed for Palestine in London, and I'm nodding and nodding and my brain is just about ready to burst into flames when all of a sudden she asks the magical question: 'I want to see the Wall. Do you think you could take me there?'

Beat, as he processes the question then comes up with his enthusiastic reply:

'We'll go right now.'

This takes her by surprise but my foot is on the pedal before she has time to change her mind. If this had been a cartoon there'd be a glowing light bulb throbbing above my head. Of course, you idiot. The Wall! The Wall is perfect. No one goes there at night.

Beat.

I drive to the outskirts of the city and park the car in a secluded spot. And now I'm thinking we could just do it in my car but she really wants to see the Wall, up close. So we get out of the car and cut through this tomato field that the Wall – or as the Israelis like to call it 'the security barrier'– just happens to bisect; leaving the irrigation wells on their side.

Chanel girl is looking up at the Wall as we approach it like it's some kind of holy relic. I have to admit that by moonlight, it looks kind of beautiful. When we reach it, she puts her hand against the concrete and a tear rolls down her cheek. 'Why can't human beings just get along?' she asks.

And I'm thinking:

thank you God,

thank you Ariel Sharon,

thank you Netanyahu,

thank you Knesset.

Thank you for giving me this moment. I hug her and say something like 'but there's plenty of love also if you care to find it.' She laughs and asks 'why are Arab men so cheesy?'

We start kissing and trying to undo our clothes gracefully. Doesn't really work in the dark. At one point, she nearly trips over her panties and I cut my thumb on my belt but still we keep going. She wraps her legs around me, I lift and hold her against the Wall and then…I enter. And it feels so good. So unbelievably, fucking good. It's like the Wall at that moment had turned into the gates of heaven and I was making love to some beautiful angel sent by God to take away all the frustration, misery and humiliation of the endless pipe dreams.

Then suddenly I'm bathed in light and for a moment I think, shit, I really am in heaven. Until I hear laughter, and someone saying hem miz'die'nim kmho ar'na'vot which is Hebrew for 'they're fucking like rabbits'.

I look up, the light is too strong. I can't see the soldiers but I can hear their laughter. Fuck, when did they put up this guard tower? In my haste, I missed it completely. Chanel girl panics, she wants to pull me out of her, she lets out a scream. I put my hand over her mouth and say 'don't move!' Her eyes are now just bulging with terror. She tries to push me again but I hold her in place. 'If we run, they'll shoot us.' I say this without stopping.

Slowly thrusting his hips.

I slow down but I don't stop.

Look, like I said: sex is really hard to come by here. I wasn't going to let those bastards ruin an otherwise beautiful night. 'But I'm British' she says 'they wouldn't dare.' I am touched by her naivety. 'Listen darling, they wouldn't give a fuck if you were Dick Cheney's daughter, they'll still shoot you. The best we could do is give them a show they'll never forget.' 'No!' she says. 'I can't do it with them watching.' I was losing her but I fought on.

Frantically.

'This is a moment where we can make a stand. Defy them. Show them that no matter what walls they build, what towers they erect, they can't stop us from living.'

Beat.

I was going to add one more thing. Thank God I didn't, it would have ruined everything. I was nearly going to say: 'let's fuck for Palestine!'

She looks at me and I could see that my words have touched her and at that moment I think fuck LA. If they don't take me, it will be their loss.

So we carry on making love against the Wall. And I hold back and hold back because I know she is having a hard time reaching orgasm with the soldiers cheering and laughing and scanning us up and down with their spotlight. I cover her ears with my hands, I feel like I'm guiding someone over hot coals. Her body tenses, her green toenails dig into my arse cheeks. She comes! I come and the soldiers grunt and cheer.

Beat.

But then..

Beat.

…they start to clap…

Beat.

…slowly at first then louder and louder and louder. Some even whistle in admiration. I do the only thing an actor could do at that moment: pull up my trousers and take a bow.

I feel her hand in mine. And this time, both of us take a bow. When she came up, she flashed the soldiers with this strange hand gesture. I thought it was a victory salute at first or possibly a peace sign.

Puts two fingers up.

It was neither.

Beat.

I drove her back to her lodgings. We sat in the car for ages saying nothing. I thought she must be shell-shocked, that the experience was too much for her.

Beat.

She had broken up with him two months earlier, she said. Nice boy, from her background, treated her good, decent. But in the end, she had to face the facts on the ground: they no longer had anything in common.

Beat.

The cropped hair was a clue but I guess my mind was elsewhere. Why do women do that, cut their hair short when they're in mourning? Is this what really drew her to Palestine, a place where her own loss could dissolve into a far greater one? I don't know, it seemed wrong to ask somehow. All I could do was hold her hand and make her promise me she wouldn't go near any willow trees or brooks and that anyway drowning herself, Ophelia-like, would be in poor taste as we have a shortage of drinking water.

Beat.

She smiled, kissed my cheek, got out of the car and ran into the convent just as the sun was coming up to the roar of an F16.

Follows the F16 then looks at the audience.

There was something anarchic about her, about Liz, that's her name. Elizabeth, like your Queen. She made me reconsider everything I thought I knew about the British.

I...I kind of fell in love with her to be honest. But then she had to go back to London to submit her thesis. I haven't heard from her since.

If you see her, tell her that the Wall is still here. She could come to visit it at any time.

2. LEVEL 42

SAJID with gold-rimmed glasses addresses the audience. His shirt could be tucked into his trousers. He's earnest, geeky almost, but has a cheeky side.

OK, this is just between us, but being in prison is just about the best thing that ever happened to me.

When I came out, it was awful.

I had grown used to the silence of the cell. Really used to it. So there I was in my parents' house, my mum fussing over me, my dad saying 'now you're a man my son' as if he suddenly lost Allah and found Kipling. And on top of that, all my mates were rushing to see me, like, well like a herd of bison. I reckon that's why the Europeans killed all the bison when they reached America, they couldn't stand the noise.

If I get off the subject, let me know. I sometimes do. Just say, 'Sajid, you're getting off the subject mate.' You don't have to add 'mate' if you don't want to. You know, if you find it beneath you. I understand. I find it beneath me too, well now that I am almost a published writer I do. It didn't bother me before....sorry, doing it again. Come on, altogether now: Sajid, you're getting off the subject mate.

Gets the audience to repeat that. Chuckles.

I made you say 'mate'!

Now, I was nine when my parents moved from Pakistan to Saudi Arabia. In Pakistan we lived in Lahore and I liked it very much. Poor as certain parts of it were, the place had culture. In Saudi, all we had were mosques and family visits to other Pakistani families.

I learnt Arabic. I learnt the Quran. I learnt to hate the Jews. It was a shit kind of childhood in so many different ways.

Then my dad got it into his head to take the money he earned in Saudi and invest it in a Pakistani restaurant in London. 'Why should the Hindus have all the monopoly?'

Still, I was glad to leave that god-awful desert hell.

Not that England was much better at first. For one thing, everyone here was listening to Nirvana.

Beat.

There is something about Kurt Cobain, that to this day, reminds me of Bin Laden. I can't quite put my finger on it. Despite my extensive research, I've been unable to conclusively prove that Cobain was influenced by Wahhabism, a hard core version of Islam.

As you all know by now I am sure, Wahhabism was invented to purge Islam of innovations considered to be sinful in the same way that Nirvana tried to purge the rock scene of the corporate image it had acquired in the 80s. To get rid of bands like…

Can't think of any then suddenly comes up with an answer:

Level 42!

Sorry, I'm doing it again. OK, altogether now: Sajid, you're getting off the subject mate.

Gets the audience to repeat that.

Well not really. See after 9/11, I started to think about Wahhabism and Bin Laden and terrorism and all that. It seemed like a fun thing to think about at the time. Everyone was doing it.

I started to go over my childhood in Saudi. Were there warning signs? Could I have seen the planes coming, so to speak?

Pleased with himself.

That's good, huh? Planes coming!

I decided that yes I could, in retrospect, with hindsight, looking in my rear-view mirror so to speak, yes I could have spotted the signs. So what better way to express my newly discovered insight into terrorism than to write a novel about it? I was determined to become East Acton's answer to Zadie Smith!

What?

But it was impossible, really just impossible to start. I had all the characters, timelines, everything worked out in my head. I even took off all the posters above my Argos desk and put up sticky yellow notes about my plot points and themes.

So why couldn't I write the novel despite my incredible organisational skills? Well because I shared a room with my brothers: Atif, Akram and Ahmad. After I was born, my dad grew lazy and only chose names beginning with A.

Beat.

So the novel stayed for a long time as a set of notes, going nowhere. It was only after I graduated from South Bank uni and entered unemployment that I found the time to finish it.

Beat.

Sajid Abdul Abdul is just a ridiculous name for many employers.

Approaches closer.

For a novelist, it's perfect. Your books are bound to be closest to the door in a bookshop. You'll scoop up all the lazy customers. Well Martin Amis and Jane Austen might give you some competition but then those two bastards always do.

Dad said I could work part time as a driver for him. Yes, the restaurant idea didn't work out because he couldn't put a menu together that was distinctly Pakistani. One day, after Friday prayer, he told me: 'son, Allah must want it this way. The Hindus have the restaurants, we have the cabs.'

Beat.

I decided to put my partial unemployment to good use. So every day after my five sisters left for their school and my three brothers bunked off theirs to sniff glue or something, I would sit in my room– trying to block out the barks of our next door drug dealer's dog – and write my masterpiece, the definitive post 9/11 novel, the one that all the others would be judged against. And I would be the man to write it. Me, Sajid Abdul Abdul Abdul.

Beat.

I didn't tell you about the third Abdul earlier because frankly I was embarrassed.

Then one day after many, many years had gone by, I typed those magic words: 'The End'. I was so happy, I cried.

I had no idea a world of pain was coming my way.

I clicked on word count and found I had written five hundred and sixty one thousand words. That's one thousand more than War and Peace.

It was a bloody epic!

So what do you do after you have written the definitive post 9/11 masterpiece? Send it to a publisher! But which one? I picked Corgi, the British publishers of Dan Brown. Just on the hunch that they must be quite forgiving.

After three days I still hadn't heard anything. I thought, that's weird. I mean I just sent them the definitive post 9/11 masterpiece, the one all the broadsheet critics keep saying hasn't been written yet and they haven't so much as sent me a text message.

By day seven, I was simmering with anger like one of my dad's experimental dishes. It's one thing to be turned down for a hotel receptionist job because your surname is Abdul Abdul Abdul but in the art world, surely there were other criteria by which a man is judged. I mean if someone spends six weeks researching which fertiliser to buy online for bomb making and after the fertiliser arrives, he goes ahead and puts a bomb together in his dad's shed just so he could describe what the fingernails of a terrorist look like, well surely such a man deserves the immediate attention of the publishing world. Right?

Shakes his head. Then speaking quickly:

By day fourteen, I thought a radical change of plan was needed. I went to the local KwikKopy and I made seventy-five copies of my novel. The girl behind the counter gave me a dirty look but I didn't care. I thought in six months' time, when my book is top of the bestseller list, she would regret not declaring her undying love for me when she had the chance. I mailed the copies to all the major publishers and also to all the major critics in all the major newspapers in Britain and when I went back home, I was so hyper, I decided to email it to them also.

He rests.

And then I waited.

Beat.

I want to take this opportunity to say that the police were really very, very nice…

Beat.

…both to me and to my family.

Beat.

The twenty German Shepherds they brought to the house did seem somewhat on the excessive side but in light of what they thought I was up to, it was understandable.

I thought the handcuffs would hurt more than they did and they were even careful to make sure I didn't bump my head when they guided me into the back of their van.

I've never been with so many white men before. It was amazing! To the left of me, to the right of me. Shoulder to shoulder. Seventeen years I've been in this country and never was I so close to any white man. And now I was with a whole squad of them. And they were all looking at me with such, such...loving intensity. Yeah, I'd like to think it was loving.

The van had no windows. But we didn't go far so I guessed we were still in London. The van doors opened and immediately I knew we were in Paddington cause the air smelled of dodginess and chips. And it was quick through a door, down a corridor, turn, down another corridor. Stop. Officer writes down my name in a ledger thing. Then off again. Horrible neon lights above, notice boards flashing by then through another door and plonk, I'm on a chair and slam, they're out of the door and I'm on my own in the interrogation room.

Minutes eek out. Time slows right down. I feel every pulse in my veins. And what starts to happen is I get a case of the panics. And it's really bad. So bad I feel faint.

What the hell is going to happen to me?

And I realise something.

I know bugger all about the law. In my novel, the terrorists get away, they escape to Pakistan. They don't get arrested. Bloody hell! When they arrested me, they said I was being held under the terrorism act. What if they put me on a plane to Guantanamo? Then I'll never see my parents again. My sisters, my brothers. I'll never get married. I'll never have a mortgage to bitch about. No, no, no, no, no, this can't be happening.

And that's when the door opens again. And in he walks. He has no name badge on and through it all, he never gave me his name. He wasn't tall exactly or muscular but meaty, you know. He had a way about him that suggested he could just lift you up with one arm and fling you across a Rugby field.

If I had to give him a name, I'd call him Bronson. He looked like a Bronson.

He drags the table right to where I'm sitting and its legs scrape across the floor. It's nails on a blackboard torture. Makes me suck my teeth.

Then he sits across from me and says.

'You know why you are here, Sajid.'

I shake my head.

'You must have a clue, surely.'

'I have no idea. I swear'

And that's when he slams my novel, all thousand pages of it on the table and says:

'I'd like to talk about your terror manual.'

And I'm like: 'What?'

'Well is that not your name on the cover? Can you deny you wrote this?'

'Of course I wrote it. I spent eight years writing it' – that probably wasn't a helpful thing to say.

'So what we would like to know is do you work for Al-Qaeda or for ISIS?'

'I work for my dad!'

'I see. And does your dad work for Al-Qaeda or for ISIS?'

And now, I'm thinking bloody hell, they're going to arrest my dad so I just burst out: 'He's not with Al-Qaeda, he's with Cuddly Cabbies!'

'Just tell me who made you write this terror manual.'

'What terror manual? This is a work of literary fiction! Honestly, it's just a story.'

'Son, if this is a story then I'll eat my boxer shorts. I'll eat them right here, right now, no knife, no fork, no ketchup, no mustard, nothing. I've been in counter terrorism since the days when Channel 4 used to be good and that's a bloody long time ago so I know a terror manual when I see one.'

And so we begin to pour over the novel, line by line, page by page. And at first I was confident that I could prove it was a novel.

'But look Arif is a character. Surely terror manuals don't have characters?'

'He's not a character. A character is supposed to have depth, an inner life, we're supposed to know what's motivating him so we can give a shit about him. Here you just have him thinking for….what? 100 pages or so about what equipment to buy so he could blow up the London Eye. That's not a story, that's just a boring shopping list.'

'It's supposed to be poetic, it's supposed to be stream of consciousness. It's supposed to be Joycean.'

But he's having none of it.

'Fuck off. You think I'm stupid? I've read *Ulysses* – well I listened to the abridged version on the radio so I know this much: at least *Ulysses* had a bit of bum licking to liven things up. This, this is dry as bag of bones gone to dust. If ISIS ran Ikea, this would be their catalogue.'

That last remark was like a dagger in my heart. But I have to admit, for a police officer, he had a way with words.

Days and days the interrogation dragged on. And slowly I began to see the novel through his eyes. And I discovered as we waded through all five hundred and sixty one thousand words that it was really, really, really boring.

It wasn't art. It wasn't. I mean I had simply thought of a very plausible terror plot where I focused far more on the mechanics of how it could be carried out than on the characters themselves. And worse there was no…no…no overall vision, no flights of fancy. It was more like reality itself. And the sad fact is that reality is not art. I thought maybe I deserve to be locked up in Guantanamo and have the keys thrown away.

But then one night in my cell, I asked myself who is Arif really? What music does he listen to? Is he into Nirvana or Level 42? By dawn, I had figured him out some more.

I asked Bronson for a pen and paper but he said he wouldn't give them to me unless I explained how my novel-slash-terror-manual ended up on the hard drive of a Jihadi bloke from Birmingham.

'I don't know. Maybe he moonlights for Corgi.' That didn't wash so I got nothing.

Undeterred, I started to rewrite the novel in my mind. All that Quran memorizing my dad made me do when I was growing up came in handy. Now that I had to compose the new draft of the novel in my head, the words had to be memorable. Masterpiece it may not turn out to be but then I wasn't aiming for that anymore. I wanted to write something that would make Bronson, whom I got to know rather well, crack a smile once in a while.

And of course in the quietness of the cell, it was so much easier to think more clearly about what I was composing.

Trouble came in the form of lawyers and other bleeding heart liberals. As Allah is my witness, as soon as word got out that a Muslim author was in a British jail, detained without charge on a suspicion of being involved in terrorism, all hell broke loose. I can tell you, much wine was spilled in Islington over discussions of my case.

I was oblivious to the hashtag free Sajid A A A campaign that was going round. I was just happy writing my new novel in my head.

It was only when the home office finally allowed my self-appointed lawyer, Geoffrey Kenilworth to visit me that I learnt all about it. But I didn't want to get out, not just yet. I didn't want to break the flow. I mean I couldn't go back home to my parents' house with its five screaming sisters and three wanking brothers, I just couldn't. But I couldn't say that to Geoffrey Kenilworth either. It would've broken the hearts of mum and dad.

So I decided I needed two stories: the novel I was composing in my head in the new style and another story in the old realistic style, one that could give the police enough grounds to keep me incarcerated for as long as I was entitled to, by law.

After the fourteen days of being detained without charge were up, the police finally charged me with being involved in a terror plot. Result!

Check it out: I told them I was the leader of a sleeper cell, biding our time in East Acton until we got the signal from ISIS to kidnap David Cameron's daughter, Nancy, and marry her off to a seventy-year-old Al-Qaeda chief in exchange for weapon grade uranium. Man, that story had everything going for it: terrorism, Sharia law, underage marriage, forced marriage, armageddon…

As if hitting a cricket ball with a bat.

It was like I'd hit a six.

But then bloody Geoffrey Kenilworth stepped in and pointed out how ridiculous the story was.

The police only managed to detain me for another week before the whole case collapsed.

The day they released me, I wept. Despite the bull I'd made up, Bronson didn't have enough to lock me up for longer. God knows he wanted to. Such a decent bloke.

Ahh, It was too short a time to complete something so ambitious.

Beat.

I wish those tossers in the house of lords had signed up to Gordon Brown's forty-two day detention without charge idea or even longer, I mean they were thinking about ninety days at one point, weren't they? Ninety days, that's three bloody months. Now that's a proper block of time for a writer. Nowadays we're only entitled to fourteen. It's not right.

I decided to get married after I got out of jail. I felt it was time.

Beat.

I did something wise. I ignored all the crazy female fans who were writing love letters to me. The letters came from everywhere: Birmingham, Leeds, Bradford, Mumbai, Lahore…even bloody Mecca.

I ignored them all.

Instead I married the daughter of one of my dad's driver mates. Aisha, named after the wily wife of our prophet. My Aisha works as a property lawyer so I guess she's wily enough for the both of us.

We've moved into a semi. It's quiet and we have a garden and everything. But you know what, it's not the same as writing in jail. It just doesn't have that romance factor. Still, I'm doing my best trying to finish the new novel, especially now with the baby on the way. I've decided to take a leaf out of Ian McEwan's book. I don't mean that literally. I mean I won't write anything more than 200 pages long, 250 max. Once you go beyond that, you're just being ridiculous. Well unless you're bloody Tolstoy.

I miss jail, I really do, some of my best passages were composed there.

Sighs.

Fourteen days, it's just not long enough.

3. THE APPLE

I like to go in about ten. Westfield. Bradford. Yeah, bro. We have a Westfield in Bradford now. Didn't you know? But get this. I'm the only one that's figured this out, I swear. I reckon, right, I reckon, they put that Westfield in there to pacify us. Stop us doing jihad. I swear I'm the only one that's figured this out. Me.

So I like to go in about ten. I'm fibbing…I'm fibbing…It's probably later…like, yeah, later. I dunno. And what I like to do…it's my thing…it's stupid…but what I like to do…is kind of creep up on it…I don't want to see it straight away, I like to creep up on it…don't ask me why…it's like, it'll be…I won't enjoy it…not if I see it straight away…I won't enjoy it…it'll be horrible…no, I like to creep up on it, little, by little…and then I see it all. The Apple Store. Wow.

So gorgeous, oh Allah it's so gorgeous. Oh come on… come on…it is..it is. That glass window? I love that glass window…I love it. I could look through it all day long, I swear I could. And the white walls…so white…it's like… it's like…

I take granddad to the mosque. Not always. Cause he goes all the time and I have a life…but bless him, I worry about him. He could fall and hurt himself so I go with him. He milks it pretending to be all invalid and stuff. He milks it but I don't mind. I go with him.

Have you been to a mosque? No? It's a matter of time. You all will, inshallah. Yeah, didn't you know? Britain is a Muslim country now. They said so on Fox TV. On Fox, they said Bradford is a Muslims-only city now. No whites allowed. I swear they did. It's madness…they must be more senile than granddad and he comes out with some right rubbish sometimes but nothing like that.

So we go into the mosque. And it's big. The main hall, it's big. Just like the Apple Store. And everyone is milling around at first. Grandad goes over to his posse, the old guard from Chakwal, and has a bit of a natter with them. And then it's sermon time and everybody snaps into line. It's like at the Apple store when they announce a new iPhone.

There is a difference though. Between Islam and the iPhone. There is a small difference. The sermons are much shorter with the iPhone.

'And what colour would you like, sir?' That's about it.

All they want to advise you on is colour and size, not how to save your soul from eternal damnation. Actually, I'm fibbing….I'm fibbing… See before you ever step into the Apple store, you probably have watched hours and hours of their sermons on your laptop. You call them ads but I call them sermons. And them sermons are snazzy. High production value. Not like the mosque sermons. The mosque sermons are pants. Sorry granddad but they are. You get some fat bloke with broken English standing at the front of the mosque and he just goes on and on and on and on and on and on and on – 'molten lead will be poured in your ear in hell, if you listen to music!!' – and on and on and on and on and on and on and on and on. And you think when is it gonna stop? And on and on and on and on. Till you start screaming inside your head 'I repent, Allah, I repent! I don't know what I'm repenting for but I repent' but still the fat bloke goes on and on and on and on. And you realise hell is not hell fire, it's that bloke never shutting up.

Na, the Apple sermons are nothing like the mosque sermons. You've seen them, the apple sermons. On their website. A short film with some cool kids on their gap year using their iPhones to help some scrawny African out in the sub-sahara. That's a sermon. Yeah, didn't you know? Course that's a sermon. But let me ask you something: What's more of a lie? That the prophet, peace be upon him, went from Mecca to Jerusalem on the back of a winged horse or that you will help some African kid when you buy your iPhone?

So I get in, Westfield, Apple Store, and I don't go to the iPhone. Uh-uh. No, not straight away. Cause it knows. Don't ask me how, it knows, it just knows, it knows I'm checking it out. I hide behind the laptops and I look at it, you know sneaky like, I give it the eye, you know...the iPhone...and it knows, course it does, it knows I'm giving it the eye. But it respects me cause I don't go up to it, not straight away. I keep my distance...it knows.

Then...then...I like to creep up on it...right up to the table, you know the white table...and I catch it by surprise. It's usually napping. When you're that close to it that's what you find. It's napping. Not like in them ads, all like swirly and stuff, no, it's napping.

And it was one time when I was this close to it that I figured it out. They put that Westfield in Bradford to pacify us, so no more lads will go over to Syria. No more joining ISIS. No more jihad. But they are fools, bro. They are big time fools.

Because the iPhone, I swear, was meant for jihad. Course it was. You've seen the footage, right? Boys my age on top of tanks. Dressed in black. Driving around some Syrian town in tanks. Doing fancy turns with tanks. And it's all filmed on an iPhone. Course it is. I think.

And now they reckon just cause they put a Westfield in Bradford, they'll stop us going over? They're mad. What's in Bradford? Why stay? Zero hours contracts. No, thanks. Loading shelves in the Ikea. No way, bro. Why waste my life here when I could be spreading Islam with an iPhone and a tank? I want the hot desert air in my face. I want to wave the black flag from the top of the tank, I want my choice of jihadi brides, you what I'm saying. I want the cool black uniform. I love that uniform.

And I want enough money to afford an iPhone. Not just dream of buying one all my life, bro.

I like to go up to it. I like to stroke the glass. I love that glass. Is it glass? I don't know what it is…but I love it. I love it. I slide my finger down and I get to that thing across the middle…you know…the fake slider and I touch it with my thumb. I like the feel of my thumb over the fake slider…argghhh, it's so…it's so…one day you'll be mine I think and then I slide it, sometime gentle, sometimes not, it changes…and you know what happens next? You know? It makes a click sound. I swear it makes a click sound. Why does it do that? There's nothing there that clicks. It's all part of their sermon, to draw you in, to drive you mad. It's the same with ISIS. There'd be no magic, right, if all they showed you were beheadings. But they're smart. They show you tanks doing three sixty, they show you lads walking around town with their AK-47s telling people what to do. The ISIS ads are full of clicks, just like the iPhone. And I dream of going over there, every day but then I think of granddad. Who'll take him to the mosque for jumma? Who'll help him with his ablutions? I can't leave him, can I? That life of jihad I could have out there, it torments me…it's like an apple on a tree, all shiny and delicious and all I have to do is reach out and grab it. But do I have the guts?

Yeah, bro, they definitely put that Westfield there to pacify us.

4. LANDING STRIP

ISSAC is boxing in a New York City gym.

I should've never sent that e-mail. Why the fuck did I do it, man? You know when you do something really stupid and then you look back. And you think. How did I not see it?

Boxes more.

When I started dating Sarah, we made love like primitive humans in a cave. But now, lately, it kinda cooled. After she met my parents, dad especially, yeah, it cooled. An intimate night now is us huddled in front of the TV, eating ice cream out of the tub and binging on Mad Men which means instead of fucking, it's like we're watching our grandparents fuck.

Anyways, me and Sarah, we seem to have fast forwarded to the cooling universe stage. Which is too soon, right? After five years, sure, but not five months. When I wrote the email, it was just cause I wanted to spice things up again. I'd had a bit to drink…OK, I was shitfaced, happy? I write to her, this columnist who gives sex advice, something like 'Dear Pam. My girlfriend's pubic hair looks like the burning bush before it burnt. Massively un-groomed. I've tried to reconcile myself to the situation but increasingly find it difficult. I would really like her to adopt a 'landing strip' style which I find very sexy and arousing. How can I get her to go along with my wish?' At this point a bang of guilt kicks in so I add: 'Or am I being too selfish? Yours, Isaac Levy.'

Click. Send. Fuck!

Next day, I read the email like a thousand times, you know with a cringing expression on my face which I always have when I read something I should've never sent.

Then about a week ago the reply arrives. Sarah was on our shared iMac and I'm walking past and I see the e-mail notice flash on the screen. My heart thumps in my chest. What if she sees the email from Pam? She'll fucking hate my guts.

So I distract her.

'You want some coffee?'

'You know I don't drink coffee.'

'Yeah, I forgot.'

'What do you mean you forgot, we've been living together for four months.'

'Yeah, yeah, I know.'

'Have you been taking horse tranquilizer again?'

'What? No!'

There was that one time, I was at a party on Long Island and…never mind.

Later when she went to see her activist friends, I printed out Pam's reply.

'Your request is a reasonable bid for heightened eroticism.' Validation. I like it. I like it.

Pam goes on: 'When there is an implied criticism – it is always best to frame your request in a loving, seductive and positive manner.' OK? And then she wrote out what I'm supposed to say. I read it and I was like…this could get ugly.

So days passed and I didn't sum up the courage. Sarah was watching a lot of TV. She's a news junky. I don't know how she can stand it. Anyways, I decide to cook a nice dinner for us: Sarah's favourite. Swedish meatballs with baby potatoes.

And I practised the words Pam said I should use.

'I always enjoy making love with you but I must confess that I fantasise about you waxing.' What the fuck, Pam? That's gonna make me sound like Hannibal Lecter.

'Would you please consider doing that because for me, the visual appeal of a "landing strip" guarantees extra excitement.' That's a mouthful. How am I gonna be able to say that with a meatball in my mouth? I should've cooked pasta.

Practices.

'For me, the visual appeal of a landing strip, guarantees extra excitement.'

Bell rings.

Shit. She's here. I open the door and immediately I read trouble on her face. She's distracted. In a daze. Those activist meetings take it out of her so I pour her some wine. We sit down at the Ikea table, eating the Ikea food. She thaws a little, smiles. Oh her smile, it just makes my day. I'm a schmuck for it. Really I am.

And so I try, I mean it's now or never. But the trouble is I don't remember Pam's words. So I improv.

Sarah, hey, listen. What, no, nothing wrong. What no! Mom is not coming over. No. It's OK. Don't panic. Thing is, you see. I wanna say…No, dad is not coming over either! I just want your landing strip to guarantee extra excitement. What? Yeah, I know that makes no sense. I know that. It's not what I wanted to say…What I wanted to say. Well, thing is, sweetheart, it would really, really, really turn me on…if…you…were..

Says the next line very quickly.

to shave your pussy so it looks like a landing strip.

Beat.

What do I mean by a landing strip? You know like a runway, like a runway on a battle ship.

And that's when all hell breaks loose. She gets up so fast, her chair flips over. Bang!

'How could you say that?'

'What do you mean?'

'How could you ask me at this time?'

'At this time?'

'How the fuck could you ask me that when children are getting bombed in Gaza?!'

Wow. Gaza? Gaza? Seriously? How the hell did Sarah manage to bring Gaza into this? How did Gaza get into our bedroom? What the fuck was she talking about?

'Sweetheart, what are you talking about?'

'We've been bombing children in Gaza for two weeks and you're fantasising about turning my cunt into an F16 landing strip?'

What the hell? I don't remember specifying the type of aircraft. Did you hear me say that? How the fuck did she come up with that?

I'm losing here. I'm losing big time. So I just want to end the conversation now. Adios romantic dinner. Arrivederci mildly perverted sexual fantasy.

'Sarah, I'm sorry. I'm sorry I brought it up.'

'Once a Zionist pig, always a Zionist pig' And with that she storms out of the kitchen and locks herself in our bedroom.

Now here we need to backtrack a little. Cause Zionist and pig are two words that might not seem well matched for each other and I see you're getting confused. Why would my nice, liberal Jewish girlfriend, hurl that kind of abuse at little old me.

Back in the day, I used to work for my dad, part time. I helped him prepare for the annual AIPAC meeting. You're all up on what AIPAC is, right? American Israel Public Affairs Committee. One of the big special interest lobbies in America like the gun lobby. AIPAC. Fuck, yeah. I loved being a part of it, man. And here is why:

My dad, his friends, practically everyone at AIPAC were street fighters in sharp suits. They had this air of manliness, even invincibility. It was dad who taught me boxing.

My job was to welcome every year to our annual conference, students from all over America. We picked up anyone who is heading for a job at Capitol Hill. We went after them and educated them about Zionism. I didn't do the educating, that was above my pay grade. But my dad, he rocks at it. He never stops boxing for Israel.

Boxes.

Say some fool decides to make a pro-Palestinian speech. Dad would come after him, swinging. First it's bangs to the body with the left hook.

He supports Hamas.

Hamas are terrorists.

At a time when we're fighting terrorists in Afghanistan, he's with the terrorists.

Terrorists.

Terrorists.

Terrorists.

But if none of that work, dad brings out the big gun.

With his right hook.

He's an anti-Semite.

Bam. On your ass, bitch. We warned you, we fucking warned you. I loved it, man. I'd be lying if I said I didn't.

We even pulled that shit against Jimmie Carter and he's a former president.

And we didn't stop with the politicians.

We went after academics too.

There was this one guy, a rising star in academia, the son of a Holocaust survivor who bangs on about Palestinian rights. He locked horns with my dad on a radio show, accused him of plagiarism. Oh, yeah, dad writes books.

Well this fight with the Holocaust dude went on and on in print, on the airwaves, on TV. The Holocaust dude even wrote a heavy tome trashing dad's book.

So when he was offered professorship at some university, Dad went for the jugular.

He worked the phones like an Indian on meth in a Bangalore call centre. He called the dean, he called the donors, particularly the Jewish ones. Played them like fiddler on the roof. He wrote to the faculty, published articles questioning the professorship choice. He even went to the campus and fired up the students.

Illustrates with boxing.

He's with the terrorists.

He makes excuses for terrorists.

He's anti-American.

But to seal the deal.

Knockout punch, upper cut.

He's a self-hating Jew.

That baby is kept special for Jews who don't toe the line. Like the Holocaust dude.

Kisses his fist.

Dad was just being dad. Dog. Bone. End of. And it worked. The university got nervous. They revoked the offer of professorship. Holocaust dude was out in the cold.

Boxes.

The thing that bothered me though is that the dude couldn't get a job anywhere else after that. He became untouchable. It must've fucked up his kids' education too.

I couldn't understand why dad went after the guy like that. It was only when I met Sarah, I figured it out.

Beat.

One day, one of our AIPAC members was supposed to be debating against this lefty organization, Jewish Voices for Peace. He injured his knee playing football and there was no one to step in so I was asked to do it. And I thought fuck it, how hard can it be.

And it was then that I met Sarah.

She was my debating opponent. And man, she was prepared. So we were starting on the history and I was on the attack. Biblical connection to the land. Holocaust, refugees, fleeing the Nazis, arriving in Palestine. The Arabs were hostile, anti-Semitic, instead of allowing the Jews to have a little country of their own, they fought and lost. Tough luck. Open and shut case.

But then she counterpunched. 'Imagine if the Mexicans took over Texas. What would the Texan reaction be? Will they take the loss on the chin and move on? How would the rest of America react, even those who post jokes about how stupid the Texans are all day long on Facebook?'

She got a lot of laughter for that. I was losing the crowd.

Then we moved onto the present and I was on the attack again. 'Hamas is a terrorist organization'. The winning mantra, right?

Sarah seemed to agree. 'Hamas is a fundamentalist, misogynistic, anti-Semitic movement that sanctifies martyrdom and glorifies death.'

'Great! We can go home now,' I said. And finally, I got a few laughs.

But then Sarah asked the audience to define terrorism. People were struggling. She then took out a fucking dictionary:

'The use of violence and threats to intimidate or coerce, especially for political purposes.'

'Here is a statement by a member of the Israeli parliament: There are no innocents in Gaza, don't let any diplomats who want to look good in the world endanger your lives – mow them down!'

'If this is not coercion through violence then what is? If both sides fit the dictionary definition of terrorism why do we only apply it to one of those sides?'

Eight. Nine. Ten. Ding. Ding.

I was kicking myself, why was I so cocky? Hell if she'd had this debate with my dad, he'd run rings around her.

I was feeling really shitty for letting the side down and I went up to Sarah in the hall outside and I said 'hey, listen, I wanna say something to you.' She stops. I look at her and it hits me – she's so fucking cute. Shit, I didn't clock that before. So then I hear myself say:

'Everything that came out of your mouth was horseshit but I'd still like to buy you a cup of coffee.'

She tells me to get lost and walks away. Then she stops, turns around and comes back. And looks at me, deep into my eyes, man and says 'I've got an hour to kill before I meet a friend. But we're splitting the tab. And, oh, I don't drink coffee.'

The first time we made love it was like rockets that had been launched against one another, banging and exploding, banging and exploding, banging and exploding. It felt forbidden. Suddenly I realized the full erotic potential of that old phrase: 'sleeping with the enemy'.

For the first time, I really read up on the conflict. And the more I read, the less sure I was about my dad's point of view.

Sarah opened up to me. She told me about a dream she had on a visit to Israel.

She dreamt about the Holocaust victims. She dreamt that their souls came out from the grounds of the extermination camps. Auschwitz. Chelmno. Majdanek. Maly Trostenets. Sajmiste. Sobibor. Treblinka. And those souls flew over the Mediterranean until they reached the Holy Land. And what those souls like to do the most was to march alongside Palestinians protesting the loss of their land.

After she told me that story, I stopped going to the AIPAC meetings. I stopped working the conferences. I got a new job and moved in with Sarah. I'm not sure why Sarah fell for me exactly but she did. Everything was beautiful between us. Until mom calls. 'We're dying to see your new girl. Come over to dinner.'

Dinner was excruciating!

Dad and Sarah clashed over everything: the environment, nuclear weapons, taxes. I was on edge the whole night. Every time, I sensed the conversation was about to drift towards Israel, I'd shift the topic. I was like the guy from the Hurt locker, except I didn't have a protective suit to shield me if the bomb went off.

I'd agreed with Sarah before we went that she'd keep schtum about her activism. But I was sweating.

Dad got to talking about the rising anti-semitism in Europe: 'Jews massacred in a kosher supermarket, People gunned down in a concert hall simply because its owners are Jewish, synagogues attacked by mobs and firebombed, banners carrying the words "Death to Jews" waved proudly.' And I was praying, just praying, Sarah wasn't going to say something dumb, bring Israel into it somehow, but Sarah simply agreed with dad. 'Considering the Shoah, it's unforgivable.' And then dad said: 'deep down all the people who pick on Israel are anti-Semites, far as I'm concerned they've got Jewish blood on their hands.'

Sarah opens her mouth. So I jump in!

'Streusel Pie, anyone?'

On the way back, Sarah was quiet. Uncharacteristically quiet. Creepily quiet. So I broke the silence.

'Say it.'

'Say what?'

'I know you're dying to say it.'

'I don't know what you're talking about.'

'It's fucked up that dad thinks critics of Israel must be anti-Semitic.'

'Ike, I'm exhausted. I just wanna get home.' The next time we made love after that, it was, for the first time, no good.

Dad was between the sheets now. And that's way worse than watching people fuck on Mad Men.

So what am I supposed to do? Wear sandals and make anti-war banners? I don't think so. I thought maybe if we spiced up the sex life, it might cheer her up.

So let's recap:

Landing strip request.

Followed by outrage and mention of Gaza.

Followed by shock from me that Gaza is now in our sex life.

Followed by storming out of the kitchen and the bedroom door slamming.

I think we're up to date.

I knock on the door. She is watching Orange is the New Black on Netflix and pretending to ignore me.

Sits on the edge of a chair.

'I'm sorry, Sarah. It was stupid to ask for that...the landing strip. Bad taste, worse timing...ever.'

I said that slowly, like I was defusing a bomb. I'm getting a lot of practice at defusing bombs.

Finally she says:

'It's time Ike. It's time we faced up to things.'

And my heart just sinks. She's breaking up with me. She met someone on the marches, maybe a Palestinian! I can't match that. I'm not the activist type, I like boxing and drinking and having fun. Does that make me a bad person?

She's breaking up with me. I see it in her eyes. And it dawns on me. I've never loved someone as much I love her.

'It's time Isaac I was honest with your dad. I can't know what I know, do what I do and keep silent just so you and I have a quiet life. I can't do it. Tomorrow is Sunday. Shabbat will be over. I want us to go over to their house. I want to tell him what's on my mind. Otherwise Ike, maybe you and I are not meant to be together.'

'I don't like threats, Sarah'

'I'm not threatening. I'm just telling you what needs to happen.'

I could feel the anger rising in me, I could feel the part of my dad, the boxer, the 24/7 boxer, rising in me. So I start packing my gym clothes. Her eyes follow me, burn a hole in the back of my neck. And I can sense the heat of her getting angry because I was about to walk out on an argument and we never did that, never.

So I made a pre-emptive strike:

'I'm not ready to be where you want me to be.' Did I scream that?

'I love my family. I don't want to lose them, why can't you understand that?'

And I leave the apartment. I get the hell outta dodge.

And so I'm here. They're about to close the gym. I've got to make up my mind what to say to her when I get back. Do we really need to rock the boat this hard? This won't be like a stupid movie. My dad is not gonna say 'I understand son' and nod and smile sagely before some soppy coda and the credits roll. This will be ugly. Very ugly. I can't do it. She's insane.

If he knows she's a leader in the boycott movement, he'll never forgive that. Especially because we kept it quiet.

You saw how he went after the Holocaust dude and that guy wasn't even dating me. Dad can forgive the Palestinians for standing their ground but he can't handle Jews turning against Israel. They're traitors in his eyes and he can show them no mercy. And I know now why that is. Because Sarah and the Holocaust dude, they're more dangerous than any Palestinian. They can't be easily ignored.

It's gonna come down to a choice between Sarah or my family. That's way too much.

He boxes with all his strength.

Fuck! I hate how life can just throw you these curveballs. Don't know up from down, right from wrong. Fuck, fuck, fuck.

Stops boxing, stands there breathing hard for a while.

What was it that Pam, the sexpert, said in her email?

Takes out the paper, reads.

'When there is an implied criticism – it is always best to frame your request in a loving, seductive and positive manner.'

Shakes his head. Looks up at the audience.

It's gonna get ugly.

THE END

THE SEVERAL BEHEADINGS OF ASHRAF FAYADH

Commissioned by West Yorkshire Playhouse,
the Gate Theatre, Notting Hill and Hull Truck Theatre
as part of World Stages Residencies.

The play was read at The Gate Theatre on 4 March 2016.
Cast: Philip Arditi, Crystal Condie and Tom Kanji.
Directed by: Tinuke Craig.

SCENE 1

Cafe. ASHRAF and a YOUTH are watching football on TV. A MAN at a distance is watching ASHRAF.

YOUTH: Who do you think will win?

ASHRAF: The foreign team.

YOUTH: We always get beaten.

ASHRAF: Our players lose heart quickly.

YOUTH: Why is that?

ASHRAF: Do you always ask so many questions?

YOUTH: Sorry.

ASHRAF: No it's good. Questions are good.

YOUTH: So what's the answer? About the players?

ASHRAF: Some say the national team reflects the nation.

YOUTH: Who says that?

> *Silence.*

YOUTH: I'm hungry.

ASHRAF: Don't you have a menu?

YOUTH: No.

ASHRAF: Here, take mine.

> *ASHRAF hands the YOUTH a menu. The MAN leaps towards them.*

MAN: What's that you've given him?

ASHRAF: Sorry?

MAN: Is that your book?

ASHRAF: What're you talking about?

MAN: You've giving this boy your book of poems.

YOUTH: *(To ASHRAF.)* Are you a poet?

ASHRAF: No, you've got it all wrong.

MAN: What do you take me for? This is clearly your forbidden book.

YOUTH: Why is it forbidden?

ASHRAF: *(To MAN.)* Sorry, who are you?

MAN: We gave you refuge. We gave you a home. And how do you repay this kindness? You hand out filthy literature to our youth.

YOUTH: Wow, filthy literature. Really?

The YOUTH flicks through the menu.

ASHRAF: It's a menu.

The MAN snatches the menu from the YOUTH.

YOUTH: Wait, I haven't finished looking!

MAN: It is a book of poems. Poems that mock God. Mock this country. Mock our values.

ASHRAF: That's not true.

MAN: Values that were handed down to us by our forefathers. Values that make this country a beacon to the world. But we made a mistake. We opened our doors for the likes of you, out of the kindness of our hearts. Because our hearts are made of gold. And you have abused that trust. You want to turn our youth against us.

ASHRAF: Look, I just came here to watch the game. I don't want any trouble.

MAN: You are under arrest, scumbag. You will go before the court. They will find you guilty. And I will take great pleasure in kicking your severed head to kingdom come.

YOUTH: Don't hurt him!

MAN: *(To the YOUTH.)* Look at the screen. Look at the bloody screen. Watch the game. Watch the national game. Don't look at him. Don't speak to him.

ASHRAF: Please, please..it's clearly not a book of poems. Just look inside!

MAN: I don't need to look.

ASHRAF: They're others like it on the other tables.

MAN: That's because you've been handing them out.

ASHRAF: It's a menu!

MAN: You think I'm a fool.

ASHRAF: Just take a look!

> *MAN flicks through the menu.*

MAN: There! That's a poem.

ASHRAF: Where?

MAN: Here where it says falafel with a dab of hummus. 'Dab', that's clearly a poetic word.

ASHRAF: It's just falafel and hummus!

MAN: It's a code. All poetry is code. You think I don't know that? You think I'm stupid because I work for the committee? Nothing gets past me, mister. Falafel is subversive food. Whether it's on a menu or in a book of poems, it's subversive.

YOUTH: Everyone eats falafel.

MAN: Shut up and watch the game.

SCENE 2

YOUTH: Who do you think will win?

ASHRAF: The foreign team, maybe.

YOUTH: We always get beaten.

ASHRAF: Our players lose heart quickly.

YOUTH: Why is that?

ASHRAF: Do you always ask so many questions?

YOUTH: Sorry.

ASHRAF: Questions are good. You should ask more.

YOUTH: So what's the answer? About the players?

ASHRAF: It's not just our players that've lost heart. We all have.

YOUTH: True.

> *Silence.*

YOUTH: I'm hungry.

ASHRAF: I have something for you.

> *ASHRAF takes out a book from his pocket, hands it to the YOUTH.*

MAN: What's that you've given him?

ASHRAF: It's nothing.

MAN: You are handing out copies of your book.

ASHRAF: I didn't know that was forbidden.

MAN: You're giving this boy your book of filthy poems.

YOUTH: Filthy, really?

ASHRAF: Sorry, who are you?

MAN: I'm with the committee for the prevention of vice and promotion of virtue. And I'm arresting you for handing out literature against god and our country.

ASHRAF: Prove it.

MAN: What?

ASHRAF: Find a line that proves what you just said.

The MAN takes the book and leafs through it.

MAN: There: 'Your heart is an idol to which your arteries have converted.'

ASHRAF: What's wrong with that?

MAN: It's a code. All poetry is code, you think I don't know that? You think I'm stupid because I work for the committee? Nothing gets past me, mister.

ASHRAF: Code for what?

MAN: To make people doubt the one and only god.

ASHRAF: Why would I want that?

MAN: Because doubting the authority of god can lead to doubting the authority of the state.

ASHRAF: So are you saying god and the state are one?

MAN: What, no, of course not.

ASHRAF: It sounded like it.

YOUTH: *(To MAN.)* I think you just blasphemed.

MAN: Your book puts corrupting ideas into people's heads.

ASHRAF: If a poem is a code like you say then you must have the key to unlock it in your mind. So if you find corrupt values in my poems there can only be two explanations. One, there is corruption in your mind that allows you to find corruption in the poem or two, there is corruption everywhere and the poem is merely reflecting that.

MAN: What?

ASHRAF: I thought nothing gets past you.

MAN: You are under arrest, scumbag. You will go before the court. They will find you guilty. And I will take great pleasure in kicking your severed head to –

YOUTH: Let him go!

SCENE 3

YOUTH: Who do you think will win?

ASHRAF: I don't really care.

YOUTH: We always get beaten.

ASHRAF: Here take this book.

YOUTH: What is it?

ASHRAF: Didn't you say you're hungry?

MAN: What's that you've given him?

ASHRAF: None of your business.

MAN: You're handing out a filthy book in a public place.

ASHRAF: Prove it's filthy.

The MAN grabs the book from the YOUTH.

YOUTH: I was reading that!

ASHRAF: Never mind, here is another.

ASHRAF gives the YOUTH another copy.

MAN: There: 'Being a refugee means standing at the end of the queue to get a fraction of a country.'

ASHRAF: Where is the filth in that?

MAN: It's seditious. It breeds discontent.

ASHRAF: I see you are not disputing the truth of the line.

MAN: Of course I am. We treat refugees with the utmost kindness in this country.

ASHRAF: And yet you want to behead me.

YOUTH: There's a poem here about breasts!

MAN: See, you're corrupting him!

ASHRAF: He was bound to come across breasts sooner or later.

MAN: You are under arrest, scumbag.

ASHRAF: *(Mocking.)* You will go before the court.

YOUTH: *(Mocking.)* They will find you guilty.

ASHRAF: *(Mocking.)* And I will take great pleasure in kicking your severed head to

ASHRAF and YOUTH: *(Mocking.)* Kingdom come!

> *ASHRAF and the YOUTH laugh whilst the MAN watches in bafflement.*

SCENE 4

YOUTH: Who do you think will win?

ASHRAF: Us, eventually.

YOUTH: But we always get beaten.

ASHRAF: That's because we live in a shit country with shit values. We wake up to shit news and breathe shit air. Our education is shit. Our rulers are shit. Shit is their thinking. What they want us to be is shit even as they say we can do better. Our TV is shit. Our newspapers are shit. Shitscared are our intellectuals. And above all, above all else. Our god is –

YOUTH: Don't say it. There's no need to say it.

> *(Pause.)*

Now what?…Why is he staring at us?…Why doesn't he come over like he always does? His silence scares me more than…Is this it? Or is he about to…? How long are we supposed to…?

THE END

IN NOVEMBER 2015, ASHRAF FAYADH,
A PALESTINIAN POET AND ART CURATOR, WAS SENTENCED
TO DEATH FOR APOSTASY BY A SAUDI COURT. AFTER
A GLOBAL CAMPAIGN, HIS SENTENCE WAS REDUCED
TO EIGHT YEARS IN PRISON AND 800 LASHES.
THIS PLAY IS DEDICATED TO HIM.